*The future is not some place
we are going to, but one
we are creating.*

*The paths to it are not found
but made, and the activity of
making them changes both the
maker and the destination.*

~ John Schaar

Acknowledgments

There are so many corporations and friends who have been instrumental over the last eighteen years in supporting the existence and mission of my organization – **Empower U** – that it would be impossible to do a proper list. So let me merely acknowledge those who had a hand in this book:

I dedicate this book to my three incredible children, Faith, Christian and Major Black. I am so grateful that I GET TO be their daddy.

I owe a huge debt of gratitude for all those on my team who keep me on course: Brett Wassell, Mark Upchurch, Tracy Bradfute, Edie Black, Lisa Hill and Valerie Kelleher. Thanks also to Bruce Eichelberger for taking all my words and making them fit together.

Finally, thanks to Eric Harvey, Steve Ventura and everyone at WalkTheTalk.com for the opportunity to do something great with their organization. I know this will matter!

180 Ways to
Live Your Life
Like It
Matters

Scott V. Black

WALKTHETALK.COM

WALKTHETALK.COM

Resources for Personal and Professional Success

To order additional copies of this handbook, or for information
about other WALK THE TALK® products and services,
contact us at
1.888.822.9255
or visit
www.walkthetalk.com

180 Ways to Live Your Life Like It Matters

ontents

To laugh often and love much;
to win the respect of intelligent persons
and the affection of children ...
to appreciate beauty; to find the best
in others; to give of one's self; to leave
the world a bit better ... to have played
and laughed with enthusiasm and sung
with exultation; to know even one life
has breathed easier because you have
lived ... this is to have succeeded!

~ Ralph Waldo Emerson

Introduction

What do you want?

That question is the key to unlocking the internal motivation in every human being. Zig Ziglar said, "You can have anything in life you want if you just help other people get what they want." It is a great quote, but I've discovered over the last twenty years that far too many people don't know what they really want in life … they're more focused on the things they *don't* want. That needs to change. Why? Because I've also learned that when one's focus shifts from what they *don't* want to what they *do* want, incredible things happen!

Successful people – people I call "leaders" – share many personal qualities. One of those traits is they live a life of purpose … they are here for a reason. When we have a purpose for being here, our lives take on a new significance … a new and vibrant passion. And, when we live our lives like that, we give others permission to do the same. We get to impact people – to build people and to help them live intentional lives as well.

Today, there is an epidemic that kills more people every year than any physical disease – and it's called **Helpless and Hopeless**. Some time ago, while being interviewed for a book, I was asked the question, "What is different about you?" I paused for a moment and said, "I see dead people." The interviewer chuckled, and asked what I meant. I explained: I see so many people walking around without passion. Dead people have no passion. They are still doing things but have separated their hearts from their activities; they have no emotional connection to what they are doing. That is truly unfortunate. But it need not be fatal. The cure: **Live your life like it matters** – because when you do, IT DOES! Once that journey begins, there is hope abounding, passion flowing and purpose persuading. Life becomes delicious, intoxicating; it takes on the qualities of a mission.

As different as we all are, we also have many similarities. With few exceptions, we all have fears and desires. We all want to love and to be loved. We all want to do good and meaningful work. We all want to be a part of something bigger than ourselves. Most importantly, we all want to know that we matter … that we are special. But here's the deal: Our "wants" can only be achieved through action. If we want to feel special, we have to BE special. If we want to leave a mark, we have to MAKE a mark. If we want a life of purpose and meaning, we have to LIVE with purpose and meaning.

Living a life of purpose is about getting stirred up for something. The opposite of being stirred up – of living a life of passion and purpose – is the contentment of "GOOD ENOUGH." We are given this great gift of life and yet so many people are walking through it doing Good Enough. Good Enough to get by; Good Enough for tenure; Good Enough for government work. They buy into the self-limiting belief that by doing things fairly well, they can stop working … stop trying. So, they do stop. They stop living their lives like they matter; they stop imagining how far, how big they can play … how many lives they can impact in a positive way. Don't be one of them!

To be sure, life can be complicated, confusing and chaotic. But it can also be passionate, purposeful and poignant. The question I always get is HOW? *How* do I make my life matter? *How* do I live a life of purpose and passion that has people remembering me long after I have moved on to a different place? I am just a store clerk, a homemaker, an auto mechanic or a junior accountant. How do I go from just an okay life of mediocrity to one that is filled with passion, vision, purpose, commitment and collaboration – one that will be remembered for an eternity? Answering those questions are what this book is all about!

As Dr. Wayne Dyer likes to say, *"Our lives are a sum total of the choices we have made."* Life is about choices. Each choice is an action step moving us in a direction. In the end, our lives will be measured by the actions we took based on the choices we made.

There is an old proverb that says: "The only way to eat an elephant is one bite at a time." And so it is with life. The only way to live our lives like they matter is one choice at a time … one action at a time … one day at a time.

> **Sow a thought, and you reap an action;**
> **Sow an action, and you reap a habit;**
> **Sow a habit, and you reap a character;**
> **Sow a character, and you reap a destiny.**
>
> – Charles Reade

Shakespeare is known to have penned, **"TO BE, OR NOT TO BE: THAT IS THE QUESTION."** I love that classic phrase, but disagree with the closing assumption. It is not a question; it is a choice … a decision. And at some point it has to be a commitment – a commitment to make today matter, to focus on making a difference, to lighten another person's burden. The only day that matters is TODAY. The only time that matters is NOW. As Jim Stovall said in *Ultimate Productivity,*

> *"Yesterday is a canceled check, and tomorrow is little more than a promissory note. Today is cash. It is real, it is tangible and you and I have to spend it wisely."*

Without question, there is much uncertainty in the world around us – a fragile economy, increased unemployment, more people struggling to get by. As a result, some folks have all but given up – losing the belief that life can, should and must be positive. In such times, we have yet another choice to make: We can focus on all the things we can't do, or do those things we can. Although we can't control what happens *to* us, we sure as heck can control what happens *within* us. That choice is yours to make.

The purpose of this book is to help people who want to live their lives like they matter. This doesn't happen by chance but by a series of steps and actions. Each day is a step on your path, and each step brings us either one day closer to, or one day farther from, being the person we were put here to be.

9

If you are committed to the ultimate goal, living your life like it matters, then you will need tools. The six foundational tools required on this journey are: Passion, Purpose, Focus, Commitment, Vision and Teamwork … all of which are described in depth in the chapters that follow.

As you read this handbook, you will find daily/weekly activities to help you live on purpose. Your life will become measured by the quality of the impact you make … not how many days you live. I do want to warn you of the dangers of actively doing the 180 activities in this book: You will find yourself with more passion and more drive in your life. You'll likely feel more energized and more appreciative of the opportunities afforded you. You have in your hands the road map to a life well-lived. What you do with this information is entirely up to you. Choose wisely. And remember …

When you live your life like it matters, IT DOES!

It's 11:59 on the Clock of Destiny
and you've only got a minute.
Only 60 seconds in it.
Didn't seek it, didn't choose it,
but it's up to you to use it.
You'll suffer if you lose it,
give account if you abuse it.
Just a tiny little minute …
but ETERNITY is in it!

~ Benjamin E. Mays
(adaptation)

Chapter 1

PASSION:
The Fuel That Makes Great Things Happen!

To the luckiest of people, a time comes when they join
or launch a cause that forever changes their lives and
the lives of others. Losing yourself in it is delicious and
intoxicating; the best word to describe the sensation
is Crusade ... Never underestimate its power. It can
transform ordinary people, products and companies
into devastating flamethrowers!

~ Guy Kawasaki, *Selling the Dream*

Passion is, at its base, about having strong feelings. The Greek meaning for the word is emotion – the indispensible fuel that propels us to greatness and triggers the power source we all have for a life well-lived: The HEART.

The best way for me to explain passion is to compare it to a candle that is burning in each and every one of us. We are born with it. As we go through life, we occasionally get knocked down ... we experience disappointment. People say they will, but they don't; he says I do, but he doesn't; she said trust me, and you find you never should have. We get hurt so we start building walls and protecting our hearts. Our candles flicker and sometimes go out. But they need not stay that way. They can be relit over and over again.

Once we reignite or stoke that internal flame of passion, fires get sparked. I have never seen a fire that didn't begin with a spark. When we can get ourselves sparked by something, new fires start within us … and they can spread rapidly.

John Wesley said, "Catch yourself on fire with enthusiasm and people will come from miles to watch you burn." When you have passion, not only will people watch you burn; they will want to burn with you!

How can you keep your candle of passion burning brightly? Here are some ways to fan your flame …

1. Choose to be enthusiastic at work today. If you encounter anyone who is being critical or negative, spread some sunshine their way. Your enthusiasm can positively affect others. Misery might love company, but enthusiasm is contagious! Help others catch it!

2. Add SOMEONE to your "To Do" list today. Interact with someone you normally don't invest your time with. What can you do to build them up? What can you do to make them feel special?

3. Develop a mission statement for your area of responsibility that answers the following: *Who are you? What do you do? What is the quality in which you do what you do?* It is important to know the "whys" behind our activities. This allows us to connect our power sources – our hearts – to our daily routines. And it can keep us stirred up and focused when things get tough.

4. Identify five things you are excited about. Write them down and read them aloud as you prepare for your day. Do this each morning and see how your week goes! When we set our "tuners" in the morning, we get better reception. Our minds are like our TV sets. When we are focused to the "excited" channel, we see more things that get us excited!

5. Do your own personal, informal 360 evaluation. Reach out to at least two of your coworkers and ask for their feedback. What do they see as your strengths? What can you do to be even better? In what areas do your passion and excitement show through? If possible, receive input from someone above you and an individual below you in your organization's hierarchy.

6. Smile while greeting people. As I have traveled the world I have learned that a smile is hello in any language. Smiles can be contagious. A smile can also be one of the greatest "Atta boys" or "Atta girls." Even if you work on the phone, SMILE; it can be heard and felt on the other end. When people are excited, they buy stuff, work harder, enjoy what they do more!

7. Develop the habit of making direct eye contact with those you are talking with. People have less trust for someone who won't look them in the eye. Also, you will be able to express your passion and enthusiasm for your job as they look into your eyes. You will see more than what people are merely saying.

8. Let your team members and senior managers know that you appreciate their support and dedication. Do it often. People want to know that they matter. Learn how they prefer appreciation to be expressed. Different people have different drivers and motivators. Make the expression of gratitude a daily habit.

9. Ponder this question: *Am I the type of person and leader that I, myself, would choose to work with?* Write out your answer. Take a look at how you lead and be honest. Are there some rough edges that you can polish? What can you be more passionate about? Identify a few specific action steps you can take to bring you even closer to who you want to be. Then, DO THOSE THINGS!

10. Focus on what you *get* to do rather than what you *have* to do. Choose to be excited about the opportunities you have today to positively affect people and outcomes. Think about the impact you can make, and notice how your passion and excitement carry you through the day.

11. Challenge yourself to "raise the bar." Set personal goals to improve your job and the interactions that are a part of your daily routine. Compete against YOU – don't compare yourself with others or wait for someone else to elevate your performance.

12. Practice emotional intelligence – exhibiting the right emotion with the right intensity, at the right time, directed toward the right person. Don't be a robot! If you work on the phone with a script, stand up and use hand gestures. Be excited about what you do and sensitive to whom you do it with. If someone is dealing with a traumatic experience, feel their pain and be understanding of their loss. Doing so will help you connect with and inspire people at an unbelievable level.

13. Don't be normal! Work at being outstanding, passionate about what you do and committed to your organization's vision and values. Get excited about your work and your life! Too many people want to blend in … to be normal. Well, they don't write books about "normal" people. Normal people rarely become heads of divisions or companies. Normal people rarely change the world or create innovation. "Normal" is a setting on the dryer!

Nothing great in the world has been accomplished without passion.

~ Georg Hegel

14. Work on agreement-gaining skills. People who master those techniques typically go the furthest in their careers. At your next meeting, have a collection of simple items – little wooden objects, toys from a kid's toy box or just common office items – and use them to encourage people to have fun, be creative and think outside the box. During the meeting, hand an item to a participant and tell them they have 45 seconds to get the participant on their left to agree to buy it. GO! You'll be amazed at the energy levels, excitement and skill reinforcement this will produce.

15. Remind yourself of your achievements. Take a piece of paper and list all the successes you have had in your life. Recall any awards, certificates, acknowledgments, accomplishments – all your successes you can remember. Keep this list by you for the next week and continue to add to it as things come to your mind. Focusing on how successful you have been will get you excited about adding to your list. It will stir you up to accomplish more!

16. Find out more about your workplace. Do a little research. Learn the history of your organization … some of the facts about how it came into being. How did the firm get started? What impact has it had in the community or the industry? Get excited about knowing more about the inception of the business and share that information with your coworkers. When we see the bigger picture of what we do, it gets the heart activated.

17. Solve problems using the right side of your brain. Brainstorming and problem-solving sessions are great ways to expand the pool of ideas for improving the bottom line. If you have a team that you work with, take them to the playground. Getting the team together to brainstorm better ways, best practices or new strategies helps build buy-in and ownership. When you can get them out of *their* environment – out of their box – the creative side of the brain kicks in, and exciting new ideas seem to show up in abundance!

18. Share your time, talents or resources with someone today. Givers tend to gain. There is a spark that takes place in our hearts when we help others. The Greek word for give is *didomi* which means "to cause something to happen." When you pass that spark along to someone else by giving to them, you can ignite a fire of desire within them. That fire can spread and stir up your passion to make a difference for even more people.

We make a living by what we get,
but we make a life by what we give.

~ Winston Churchill

19. Find someone in your life who demonstrates passion in their field of endeavor. Interview them; learn from them; find out why they are so excited about what they are doing. Examine their daily behaviors – and work on replicating them yourself. Remember that passion is contagious. Studying the passion in others will likely spark more passion in YOU!

20. Identify what activities you do that bring the greatest worth or value. At the end of a week, write down all the activities you performed. With all you did, what were the most important and meaningful things? Identify the top two to four activities, and jot down the underlying WHY for each. What is it about those activities that provide value? The answers will illuminate a deeper desire for – and commitment to – your mission. Use this information to get more passionate about what you "get to do!"

21. Consider what a perfect customer experience would be like. How would the customer feel about the interaction? What level of excitement would he or she notice? What would the server do to ensure the customer's satisfaction? Use that mental picture as your guideline for serving others.

22. Today, bring fire to all your interactions. Passion is the fire that burns to greatness. In emails, conversations and interactions, remind people how lucky you (and they) are to be important parts of your organization. Get your fellow team members sparked about the many opportunities available to impact people with your products or services. Help others see the bigger picture and encourage them to become emotionally involved with everything you do! Infect others with your passion. When people get excited, great things happen!

23. Identify the things about your job that you like the most. Staying focused on what you enjoy keeps your passion and enthusiasm on the surface for all to see. And consider how you might bring some of that passion to your less desirable tasks. Every activity has some positive aspects connected to it. Identify them … stay focused on them … appreciate them.

24. Think about what your "Loyalty Meter" is reading. Question whether or not those you work with, and for, can SEE how loyal you are to the enterprise. Do you appreciate working for your organization and team? Do you wear the company's logo with pride? Do you represent the business at community events? How might you demonstrate more loyalty to the team, to an individual or to the company? What are some ways that loyalty shows up in the daily routine? What can you do to demonstrate more loyalty and give others permission to do the same?

If there is no passion in your life,
then have you really lived?
Find your passion, whatever
it may be. Become it, and let it
become you and you will find great
things happen FOR you,
TO you and BECAUSE of you.

~ T. Alan Armstrong

Chapter 2

PURPOSE
Why Are You Here?

*Man does not simply exist, but always decides what his
existence will be, what he will become in the next moment.*

~ Viktor Frankl

Most of us have heard the saying about the journey of a thousand miles
beginning with a single step. The truth is: it begins with a single step and a
road map. That road map is your purpose.

Purpose explains the why behind everything – why you are here, why
you are doing what you are doing, why you are going where you are
going. Although I don't agree with many of Nietzsche's teachings, I do like
this quote of his:

"He [or she] who has a why can bear almost any how."

If posed with the question, "Why are you here?" could you answer clearly
and definitively? Beyond the typical "to work and take care of my family"
explanation, why are you occupying this body at this time, on this planet?
Why do you do what you do at work? You could be doing anything, but
you are not … why are you doing what you do?

Purpose explains why you are on your journey so you can understand which way to go. It also helps as you maneuver through the daily choices you continually make. As the Cheshire cat told Alice inside the looking glass, "If you don't know where you are going, any road will get you there!"

Purpose provides direction – while vision lights the way, team builds strength, commitment steadies the course, focus steers the ship and passion creates the energy. Purpose is your road map for making a life that matters. So, today ... this week ... this month: choose to live a life with more purpose. Here are some ways to make that happen ...

25. Find some quiet, special place on a weekend and dig deeper into the bigger picture. Ask the questions, "Why am I here ... what am I meant to do?" This is beyond your work, perhaps beyond your family. It is a deeper connection to this life. Write out your thoughts and notice how that affects everything you do at work and at home. This deeper connection will allow you to be more emotionally involved with everything you do.

26. This week find one thing that you can do to give of yourself. Preferably it is not something you have done before or are currently doing. Go to a homeless shelter and feed the people; go to a nursing home and spend quality time with one of the residents. Jump in and help a coworker with a difficult task. Afterwards, reflect on how it made you feel ... what you got from giving of yourself.

27. Review your organization's mission and consider how you might better contribute to it. Do you have a written mission statement? Is there an employee handbook? Take a look at your area of responsibility and see how you can be a part of the bigger picture. Why do you do what you do? Hopefully it is for more than merely a paycheck.

28. Enroll in a personal improvement course. Make sure it is either job specific to what you do or a general leadership development program. Let others see that you are working to be the "best of the best." It can be contagious.

29. At the end of each day, or project, or week: replay your performance. Take an inventory of what you did well, and what you can do better. Learn from your successes and from those things you didn't handle that well. As you consider all your activities, where do you see potential areas of improvement? Truly effective people wear an invisible sign that reads …

> **UNDER CONSTRUCTION:**
> Working to be better today than yesterday –
> and better tomorrow than today!

30. Create a new habit today. Pick one thing that you have wanted to do better or a new behavior you want to add to your daily routine … maybe it is getting up earlier in the morning so your day goes better, or choosing to have a happier, more positive outlook. Commit to do it for the next thirty days. Aristotle said, "We are what we repeatedly do." Who are you?

31. Write out your eulogy. A eulogy is the wonderful, nice, positive things someone says about you when you are not alive to hear them. It summarizes the way you lived your life, the things you accomplished and the impact you had on those around you. If you lived your life to its fullest potential as a leader, a coworker, a family member, a friend and a citizen, how would YOU be remembered? At times we need to refocus on who we are and why we are here. One of the best ways to do that is to begin with the end in mind. It is ok to be emotionally involved. Why were you here? What was your purpose?

32. Take inventory of the special skills and talents you have been blessed with. What are the things you do particularly well – perhaps better than most other people. Where do you excel? What seems to just come naturally to you? Chances are that your overall purpose in life can be found woven within these wonderful gifts that make you unique … that make you who you are.

Whatever you are by nature, keep to it; never desert your line of talent. Be what nature intended you for, and you will succeed.

~ Sidney Smith

33. Consider all the roles you perform in your work environment. Identify one or two ways you can "do better" in those roles. Are you a leader, a cheerleader, a counselor, a salesperson? Identify all the "hats" you wear in your job environment and then commit to enhancing your performance in each of those roles. Ongoing self-development is one of the keys to living a purpose-based life.

Along that same line …

34. Read about others who have succeeded in your field of endeavor. The road to success can be bumpy and have many obstacles. When we can learn about how others have overcome challenges and what choices they have made to do so, we can be confident and encouraged about our own journey. So get a book about somebody whom you respect or admire and find out about them … and learn from their experiences. What was *their* purpose and how did *they* fulfill it?

35. Solicit feedback from someone you lead – a team member who answers to you, either directly or indirectly. See how you might be able to lead them better. Explore what you could do differently to help them be more successful. Ask what you could do to better contribute to their success.

36. Help others while you are on the road. Start collecting all the soaps, lotions and shampoos that you have in your hotel rooms. Take these items (that you really don't need) and put them in your suitcase. There are homeless and women's shelters that these items can be donated to for their temporary visits. Add more purpose to your traveling than merely going somewhere.

37. Make sure you acknowledge those who are behind the scenes making things happen. Remember it takes a team. Maybe it's the receptionist for the client you are calling on, or perhaps it's someone in your maintenance or information technology department. Acknowledge those that usually receive little notoriety. You might make someone's day – and that's a great purpose to serve.

38. Acknowledge those around you. Don't let people feel invisible – as if they do not matter. Whether it is a "walk-in" customer, the receptionist or the janitor; when people know they matter they act differently. Greet people when you get to work in the morning. If a customer comes in, acknowledge them and say hi. Make one of your "purposes" to show people that they are recognized and they matter.

39. Keep a goal log. Write down all the personal goals you set for yourself and your team. Keep track of your status – goals that have been achieved and those that are still in progress. Review your list at the start of each day. You'll stay focused on getting results and begin every day with an important reminder of the purpose of your efforts and activities.

40. Practice listening! One of the characteristics of great leaders – and great people – is a willingness to listen to others. Too many people only listen for an opening for rebuttal … for their chance to say their piece. They fail to hear and understand what the other person is saying. If you've ever experienced that, you know how demotivating it can be. When we listen to people, we demonstrate respect. We hear their concerns, their motivations and their needs. Listen on purpose – *with* a purpose: to UNDERSTAND another human being. You can't make your own life matter without showing others that they matter as well.

41. Are you going to the goal line or the stands? When you set goals, try your very best to *exceed* them rather than merely meet them. People appreciate us meeting their expectations, but they really get thrilled when we go beyond what they expect. When it comes to collaboration and service, is your purpose to create satisfied internal and external customers or "raving fans"?

42. Check your "purpose focus." Take a piece of paper and write down all the purposes for and in your life. What were you put here to do? What's your role … your mission … your *raison d'etre?* Take your time. List as many things as you can. Then review your list, and circle all the items that involve contributing to the betterment of other people (rather than yourself). Are the majority of the items on your list circled? If so, you have a terrific road map for living a life that matters. If not, work on adjusting your focus more toward others.

I expect to pass through life but once.
If, therefore, there be any kindness I can show,
or any good thing I can do to any fellow being,
let me do it now, and not defer or neglect it,
as I shall not pass this way again.

~ William Penn

43. Practice walking in someone else's shoes. Not literally, just figuratively. Demonstrate the value of empathy. If you want to connect with someone, then you need to understand their map of reality. Unless you know the struggles or the stresses of a certain job and the demands of that job, you can't really understand how to help them do better. Dr. Robert Rohm, an expert on team building, had a saying that I have adapted:

"If I can understand you a little better, and you can understand me a little better, doesn't it make sense that we are in a position to have a better relationship?"

44. Under Promise and Over Deliver! Whenever you promise something, document it – and make sure you do more than that! People will always remember what you promise and what you do. So, do more than you say you will. Never make a commitment unless you are going to do it. This by itself will help you enjoy a life well-lived!

45. Become a note taker extraordinaire! When having conversations or attending meetings, make a habit of taking notes. It shows that you are involved with what is going on and ensures that you will remember what needs to be done. There is only so much space in our "Random Access Memory." You won't be able to remember everything, but you can write things down for future reference. Remembering all the things that matter helps you live a life that matters.

46. Learn by teaching. One of the best ways to learn something new is to teach it to someone else. If there is something you want to learn in your organization, volunteer to teach it. If there are new rules, a new software program, a new initiative – see if you can teach it to the rest of the team. Not only will you show your willingness to be a team player, you will also master that thing that you are teaching!

47. Write out a handwritten note or card and mail it to someone. In the electronic age in which we live, most successful people have hundreds (if not thousands) of emails in their inbox. Separate yourself from "most"; reward someone in a way that will keep on giving. That handwritten card or letter – once it is read – is often put on a desk or a wall, or made a keepsake. People will remember the extra effort you put forth and know that one of your purposes in life is to think of others and make them feel appreciated.

48. Show up to a ballgame, a recital or an event for a family member of one of your work associates. It will show your commitment to your team and their successes. It will also help you understand your associates better by seeing a fuller picture of who they are.

49. Help a coworker, family member or friend get something they want. Find out what someone needs or would like to have, and take action to help them get it. Attach no strings to your effort. Do it simply because it's what good leaders – good people – do!

Similarly …

50. Put together a work team to help out an employee, team member or a family member of a coworker. When we remember that our work associates are people with families who also have needs, it shows that we are caring individuals. Paint a house, clean a yard or organize a small food drive. Activities that invest in people who are part of the organization increase the dedication and loyalty of people *to* the organization. And it's a great, purpose-driven way to use your time and talents.

51. Do a behavioral audit. Identify how and where you spent your time and money over the last three to six months. If you want to know what's really important to someone, don't ask them – watch what they actually do. So what's been getting your attention, your efforts and your financial resources? If someone did not know you, what conclusions about your life purpose might they make based on the data? Is that how you see yourself ... how you want to be seen?

52. Reflect on those people who have made the biggest impact on your business life. Who has mentored you, taught you, led you and inspired you in your career? Identify three people who have influenced you the most and write out the impact they have made. Then, write a personal note to each describing the results of their investment – and thanking them for making one of their purposes in life to help you. Finally, commit to honoring these people by paying their gifts forward to others.

53. Make today count! Take 30 minutes of time before work today and write out ways you will make a difference for others. Will you open a door for a stranger, help someone change a frown to a smile or spend some extra time with someone in need? Every day you have the chance to be a difference maker. What will you do today to make a difference in your section, in your department at your place of work? See how many ways you can make it matter that you are living at this time and working at your organization.

54. Dress for success. There is a term used in the fields of leadership and goal setting: "as if." AS IF is a great way to move from where you are to where you want to be. If you start dressing AS IF you are successful, you will feel more successful. And that affects your confidence and the way you view yourself. Commit to maintaining a successful, professional appearance and notice how you feel ... and how others treat you.

*I think the purpose of life is
to be useful, to be responsible,
to be honorable,
to be compassionate.
It is, after all, to matter: to
count, to stand for something,
to have made some difference
that you lived at all.*

~ Leo C. Rosten

Chapter 3

Focus:
The Law of Attraction

The tragedy of life doesn't lie in not reaching your goal.
The tragedy lies in having no goal to reach.
It isn't a calamity to die with dreams unfulfilled,
But it is a calamity not to dream.
It is not a disaster to be unable to capture your ideal,
But it is a disaster to have no ideal to capture.
It is not a disgrace not to reach the stars,
But it is a disgrace to have no stars to reach for.
Not failure, but low aim is sin.

~ Dr. Benjamin E. Mays

I once heard that the quantity of available information doubles every year. Frankly, that is too much to learn. We can't know everything, but we can learn to focus on what is truly important!

We have an incredible ability to focus. But staying focused is another matter entirely. A newborn baby can grab hold of something attached to our bodies and squeeze and hold onto it with incredible strength. Even though the infant has very little muscle tissue, it's tough to pry those little fingers loose. But only jiggle a rattle or a set of keys off to the right or left, and that baby will easily change focus and release his or her grasp. Adults are no different. When we lose our focus, we lose our grip. And if that happens, we diminish our ability to reach our true potential.

In order to live a life that truly matters, we must be fully present in the NOW moment ... we must learn to unleash the power of focus. Why? Because our brain stem has a section called the Reticular Activating System (RAS). It is the brain's focal center, and whatever we focus it on, we tend to move in that direction. A few years back Rhonda Byrne wrote a book, *The Secret*, which speaks to that very phenomenon.

We are made incredible creatures. We have our eyes in the front of our face for many reasons. One of the reasons is that we tend to look in the direction we are moving and move in the direction we are looking. Our focus dictates our direction in that moment, that hour, that day ... in our lives. The challenge we all face: to maintain a laser-like focus on our purpose, our goals, our beliefs and the important tasks at hand. Fact is: you can't hit the bullseye unless you keep your eye on the target!

Here are some focus-related action items to try ...

55. Sit down and write out what is going on in your head. What are you thinking about? What are you worrying about? What has your attention at this very moment? Journaling is a powerful way to clear our minds of things that challenge our ability to focus. If you want to change your life, change your thinking. The reason why so many people have a hard time focusing is because of internal dialogue. Take 15 minutes of quiet time to examine what's in your head. Writing things down will allow you to focus on what you're focusing on – and determine if your mind is in the right place.

56. Help make the most of each activity through preparation. When a meeting, discussion or event is on your schedule, be prepared. Do your homework; look up the topic; find out about the pros and cons; educate yourself so you can be ready to actively participate in whatever process is involved. Remember that preparation brings focus, and focus leads to success.

57. Write down five things that are good and positive about your life and/or your job. Review that list often as a reminder. Avoid the temptation to focus on how unfair things may seem at any given moment. When we take control of our focus and concentrate on what's good, our perspective changes. The mind cannot hold two opposing viewpoints in the same space. It is impossible to be positive and play the "victim" at the same time. If we want to live a life of value, we must consciously control our thinking.

> *"We can always choose to perceive things differently. You can focus on what's wrong in your life, or you can focus on what's right."*
>
> ~ Marianne Williamson

58. Today, do something different. We sometimes get into ruts and patterns – and we can become stagnant. We start going through the motions. When you drive to or from work, take a different route. Get dressed differently; handle a situation a little differently. Get out of the box. No true growth takes place in our comfort zones. See how you can journey outside that comfort zone and be aware of how that affects you. Is the autopilot running?

59. Manager or leader? You decide! Identify your leadership and mentoring patterns, and consider whether you are being more of a manager or a leader. Managers manage *things;* leaders lead *people.* Managers do things right; leaders do the right things. Managers and leaders both play important roles. You need to decide which role you play and focus intently on doing it the best you can.

60. Move something out of the impossible to the possible. Identify a task, activity or goal in your work life that you have not dealt with because you thought it couldn't be done. Maybe there is an issue, a process or an opportunity that you never gave credence to. What if it *was* possible? What would the first few steps be to move in the direction of success in that endeavor? Now, focus on them. DO them, and see what happens.

61. Identify some trial in your life and reframe it. Many people learn far more from struggles and failures than they do from their successes. Reframing allows you to change the meaning of an event or circumstance. Consider how this obstacle or problem is helping you grow and become stronger. How might this be an opportunity in disguise? What can you learn?

62. Focus on having some fun. Program things that bring laughter and enjoyment into your weekly schedule. Our minds need to be periodically refreshed and revitalized. Most people have more clarity, creativity, problem-solving ability and overall emotional intelligence when their brains are NOT in a vice grip! When not abused or overdone, fun is positive, therapeutic and contagious.

63. Be aware of what you listen to and conversations you engage in. Sometimes negative things can be easier to talk about than positive ones. Before you know it, the environment can become counterproductive and even turn caustic. If you find yourself in the middle of a negative or gossipy situation, ask:

What can I do to turn this around?

Someone needs to encourage people to focus on, and talk about, more positive things. If not you, who? If not now, when?

64. Catch someone doing something right. Sometimes the only time people hear from us is when they have done something wrong – because that's where our focus tends to be. Look for ways and opportunities to acknowledge people for the good things they are doing – including any improvement you might see. They will appreciate the praise and want to continue to do better.

65. Stay focused on where you are at any given moment. When at work, try to be 100% focused on job activities. Keep the personal phone calls and emails to a minimum. Concentrate on being the best employee in the NOW moment. When you leave work, LEAVE WORK! Change your focus. When interacting with those at home, give them 100% of you too.

66. Keep a food journal. Take a week and focus on the various foods you eat. Every morsel we put in our mouths impacts our energy and our moods in some way or another. Proper nutrition (or the lack of it) affects both our physical and mental capabilities. Do you tend to "crash" a few hours after lunch? Are your mornings sluggish – requiring an hour or so to "get into" your work? Do you pay attention to – and make choices by – the information on food labels? Consider what you eat and notice how healthier meals allow you to be more productive and focused on being the best you can be!

67. Make it difficult to get distracted. Distraction, by its most basic definition, is a loss of (or disruption to) attention and focus. We all face it, and some of us find ourselves sidetracked more easily than others. So make an effort to minimize the potential for distraction that you may experience. Handle email a few times during the day rather than responding as each is received. Clear your work area of things that are not related to the specific activity you're performing. Remove the games and social media from your computer – or make it more difficult to access them. The fewer distractions you encounter, the easier it will be to stay focused on what's truly important.

68. Use TO-DO lists. Write down all the things you need to focus on and accomplish each day. Next to each item, write the time you feel it will take to complete it (be realistic in your estimates). Then prioritize your list – identifying each item as high-, medium- or low-priority. Next, add up the estimated times for completion. Based on the time total, remove or add lower-priority items until your list is realistic and doable. Finally, FOLLOW THE LIST – checking off items as you complete them. Work on developing your focus discipline by saying to yourself: "With the exception of unexpected emergencies (or significant opportunities), if it's not on the list, I won't allow myself to get side-tracked with it."

69. When you get complimented for doing a good job, dig deeper. Ask the person for specifics. Inquire about exactly what it was you did that was noticed – and why it was appreciated. Make note of what is said to you, and commit to doing more of it more often. Focus on what is said, and put it in your toolbox for later use.

70. Speak more positively! Examine the words you use and get rid of those which are tentative ("wishy-washy"). Our words can actually program our actions and the actions of others. Make a conscious effort to get rid of some words and minimize the use of others. For example, *try* is a word the graduates of our training programs learn never to accept! There is no commitment when we merely attempt. To quote Yoda, "Do, or do not. There is no try." Our customers and team members don't appreciate words like *Shouldda … Can't … Won't … Maybe … Impossible … Sorry.* Work to be positive and committed in your vocabulary with words like *Yes … Will do … Absolutely … You bet … I'll get right on it!*

71. Focus on potential solutions, not just problems. Sometimes we can get so caught up wallowing in what is wrong that we tend to see only bad stuff. Condition yourself and your team members to be more solution-oriented. When thinking about a problem or communicating it to someone else, add these words to the end of your problem description: "and here's what I think we should do about it…" If one of your team members comes to you with a problem, listen intently and then ask, "What are some things we might do to resolve this issue?"

> "Don't dwell on what went wrong.
> Instead, focus on what to do next.
> Spend your energies on moving forward
> toward finding the answer."
>
> ~ Denis Waitley

72. Stop taking yourself so seriously! Make a commitment to laugh at yourself and focus on the hilarity of life. We can sometimes get so bogged down in doing, putting out fires, taking care of everybody and everything that we forget to laugh. Laughing releases different chemicals that help us function with clarity. Find a funny web clip, a funny show or something that just tickles your funny bone, and laugh. Then notice how much more productive and enjoyable your days become!

73. Don't go crazy! Focus specifically on something you seem to be getting nowhere on or with. It can be a task, an employee issue, managing a project or anything else that has you frustrated. Regardless of how you have been dealing with it, change your approach. Do something different. Einstein told us that the definition of insanity is doing the same thing over and over and expecting different results. If you don't like results you're getting (or not getting), focus on a new approach.

74. Focus on what you want for your life and your career. Knowing what you want is one of the best ways to personally motivate yourself. Take a piece of paper, and at the top of the sheet write, "I WANT…" Then begin writing for three to five minutes. Do not analyze, cross off or edit your responses. RUSH WRITE. Write nonstop and see what comes out. Once finished, clear your head, grab a new piece of paper and do the process again. See what new stuff comes out. What did you learn about your needs and desires? What did you learn about yourself? What, specifically, will you do to turn your *wants* into *haves*?

75. Reflect on the things about your job that you like the least. You need to identify these "Golden Gripes" in order to do something about them. Once you identify them, strategize different ways that you might affect change in those areas. Has anyone else faced similar concerns that you might learn from? Should you talk with your manager or someone in another department? What can you do to improve the work environment? These "Golden Gripes" take away from our passion and enthusiasm. Take whatever action you can. If you find that something can't be changed or improved, accept it and focus on the things you do enjoy!

76. Focus on your PDA! With few exceptions, Public Displays of Appreciation build individual self-esteem and increase the desire to achieve more. Publicly acknowledging people not only shows that you appreciate them; it also affirms them in the eyes of others. I had a team member once tell me that she had heard me compliment her before, but when I said what I said publicly, tears started flowing from her eyes! So, make sure recognition is warranted. When it is, acknowledge people; thank them; brag about them; celebrate their accomplishments and contributions in front of others.

77. Identify the acknowledgment perceptions you have about your job by answering the following questions:

In what ways am I appreciated at my job?
I am shown my value as an employee by ...
My opinion is sought out in the following ways ...
I am acknowledged as an important team member by...

Once you have answered these for yourself, answer them for the people who work for you. What is it that YOU specifically do to let your coworkers know that they matter? The basics of human relations teach us that any behavior reinforced with a positive outcome will repeat itself. With the information you acquire from these questions, consider what behaviors you need to focus on to make sure your team is effectively reinforced.

78. Have a "Mission Meeting." Get your entire team together and write out a department or TEAM mission statement. The pieces of a mission statement are:

> Who you are.
> What you do.
> The quality with which you do it.

Not only will this help keep your team focused on their purpose, it will also create "buy-in" and an ownership mentality for their areas of responsibility. When people get to be part of the process, they seem to be more committed to the outcome!

79. Organize, or be a part of your company getting involved with, a charity and physical fitness simultaneously. 5K runs, building homes for the needy, etc. provide excellent opportunities to connect with your team outside of work, encourage improved health through physical activity and make positive contributions to people and causes.

80. Write a letter from a "Raving Fan." If a customer or someone on your work team were to write out a testimonial based on the experience you want them to have, what would they say? This is a great way to clarify your service expectations. Ken Blanchard says that "Raving Fans" are so pleased with the service or product that you gave them, they sell you to others – based on their experience. If you lead a team, have them write similar letters. You'll help them focus on providing great service, and you'll have a better feel for what they believe is expected of them.

81. Take responsibility for your mistakes. If you are "playing big" and making a difference, you are going to make mistakes. When that happens, own up to it! No matter if you're dealing with a customer, a coworker, a family member or a friend – admit the error, apologize for it, fix it, learn from it and then move on.

82. Create a mental space that allows you to be the best possible you! Block off several minutes for this. You will need solitude, some relaxing instrumental music and something to write with. Envision the "perfect place" (an ocean front, mountain top, desert oasis) where you can get away from any stresses that are squeezing you. Close your eyes. See your place. Hear it. Feel it! The more vivid the colors, clearer the sounds and descriptive the items you can feel, the more real and the more effective the tool. Once you have the details down, write them out. Better yet, draw a picture as a reminder. Next time you find yourself having a bad day, take a few moments to mentally travel to this great space and get yourself in a better state of mind so that your friends and family get the best you … not the leftovers. When you have a bad morning before work, go to this place and get your head on straighter so your coworkers get the best possible you!

83. Commit to achieving a goal that you have wanted to accomplish but haven't yet. Approach that goal with a three-step process:

1. Want it. 2. Create it. 3. Live it.

Reflect on the "why" behind the goal. What need or desire does it fulfill? Then, with the end in mind, create it mentally. When you accomplish this goal, what will it look like, sound like or feel like? Finally, formulate the plan to live it … to make it happen! Identify the first several actions you are going to take to move you in that direction. Track your success and be prepared for the next action items. Doing all of this will help you stay focused on your goals … and achieve them!

84. Take a lesson from Ben Franklin. Leaders need a sound decision-making strategy. When decisions need to be made, do what Mr. Franklin did. Take a piece of paper and draw a vertical line down the center. On one side write "Pros," and on the other side write "Cons." List all of the pluses and minuses you can think of for the decision you're considering. Then count the numbers, weigh their potential impacts and importance, and then make your decision based on what will provide the most "pros" for the most people. Doing so helps eliminate feelings from the process and keeps your focus on the facts.

85. Turn your vehicle into a classroom. If you drive as part of your job, use that time wisely. You can "Grow as you go!" Get a leader-ship book, professional journal or autobiography on CD. Then listen and learn as you drive. Imagine the hours of growth and education you can gain through job-related travel.

86. Look for an opportunity to interact and work with someone "new." Get involved with an interdepartmental project, volunteer for a committee or help plan and coordinate a new initiative for the business. You learn new things from new people – and build new relationships.

Only when your consciousness is totally focused on the moment you are in, can you receive whatever gift, lesson, or delight that moment has to offer.

~ Barbara DeAngelis

Chapter 4

COMMITMENT:
It's the GO Button, Baby!

No horse gets anywhere until he is harnessed.
No stream or gas drives anything until it is confined.
No Niagara is ever turned into light and power until it is tunneled.
No life ever grows great until it is focused, dedicated, disciplined.

~ Harry Emerson Fosdick

Many people confuse participation with commitment. A great way to explain the difference is by way of a chicken and a pig – and a morning meal of bacon and eggs. In that breakfast, the chicken participated but the pig was totally involved. What is the difference between giving an egg and giving your whole self? Commitment!

I frequently joke that we should all file a class action suit against one of the national office supply chains (and I *really* am kidding when I say that). For years they have been using a big red button labeled "easy" in their marketing materials. You can actually buy the button and press the heck out of it. But your life won't change. There are no shortcuts to success. It takes effort, action and commitment.

Instead of an EASY button,
what we all need is a GO button!

Everybody reading this book either has kids or was a kid at one time. Remember those slot race tracks? We would snap sections together – connecting a slot that ran through the entire track. Some were figure eights, some were ovals and some had "loop-de-loops." We would then take our little race car with a metal post sticking out the bottom and slip the post into the slot in the track. Finally we would attach the wires of the controller – typically a handle grip with a button or trigger-type lever. There was no steering wheel – just a single button. When we pressed the button, the car went wherever we laid out the track.

Slot cars are a great metaphor for life. You have a track that is laid out when you have vision and purpose. To get your motor running, you just have to press the GO button. The GO button makes things happen. It brings energy to the track and makes things go. The GO button for all of us is COMMITMENT! So make a personal commitment to applying the information you read in this book. Commit to living your life like it matters – because it does.

Remember those slot race tracks. Press the GO button. Get your motor running!

87. Make sure that your word is your bond. If people cannot trust you with the small commitments, how will they be able to trust you at all? Be careful about giving your word, promising or committing to do something unless you are "all in."

88. Make a commitment to continuous learning. Knowledge is power. Find something you are interested in, passionate for or curious about – then read a book or take a class on that topic. Our brain is the only organism that does not have to wear out. We can keep young and fresh by continuing to expand our base of knowledge.

89. Do something today that makes you better at what you get paid to do. If you are in sales, make five extra calls. If you are a technician, find some online information that will help you be more efficient. In order to truly live your life like it matters, you need to take full advantage of opportunities to make your performance, each day, better than the one before.

90. Get involved at work *beyond* your work. Many organizations have projects, task forces, committees and other similar opportunities for employees to work outside of their normal, everyday jobs. Find something that you believe in or enjoy and get involved. Let your commitment show by giving of yourself to help make things better for everyone.

91. When finished with a big project, an important task or an activity for which you volunteered, solicit candid feedback from those you worked with and for. In order to reach our true potential, we need to know what we do well and what we need to improve upon. Consider posing these two questions to your feedback providers:

> 1. What was it that impressed you most about my performance?
> 2. If you had to identify two things I could do to improve my performance in the future, what would they be?

92. Make a health commitment to take better care of yourself and get your body moving. What good is it to create a great life if you are not around to enjoy it? Start an exercise program and stay with it. Begin slowly so you can experience initial success and avoid wearing yourself out. Find a workout partner who can encourage you – and make sure you return the favor. You will feel better, have more energy and ensure that your life matters!

93. Commit to put extra effort into your work! Whatever you do today, do it like it was a final exam ... as if "getting a job" depended on it. Take pride in it, go the extra mile, give it all you have. John D. Rockefeller said, "The secret to success is to do the common things uncommonly well."

There are only two options regarding commitment. You're either in or out. There's no such thing as a life in-between.

~ Pat Riley

94. It's okay to *beat* the schedule. Try being "early" on deadlines, goals and project completions. When activities are well organized and accomplished ahead of schedule, it speaks volumes about your commitment and management skills. Be prepared ... be early ... be noticed! You show up well when you show up early!

Similarly ...

95. It's okay to hurry. Just for one day, live with a sense of urgency – except while driving. Walk at a faster than normal pace ... get a swing in your gait. Live your day out like you were on a deadline. The time is NOW! Move with alacrity; interact with alacrity! Live it with Passion – Heart, Body and Soul. At the end of the day document: How did it make you feel? How productive were you? What effect did it have on those you interacted with? How will you apply this information?

96. Identify your goals for the week. People don't plan to fail, but they do fail to plan. Some don't set goals … others fail to write them down. Be exceptional – be a goal-getter! How will you know if you had a successful week or not? Begin with the end in mind. What are the things you want to accomplish? Write them down and monitor them.

97. Move from the urgent to the important with your focus and activities. Choose a time when you can "rewind" your past week (or day) and jot down all the things that you invested your time in. Now go through and categorize each activity. Was it "urgent" (you felt you needed to handle it immediately), was it "important" (it's directly related to your mission and overall success) or was it both? Write a "U, I or U/I" next to each item. Now, analyze your list. Did you spend the majority of your time on those things that were merely urgent, or did items with importance connected to them get most of your attention? If it's the former, consider making some adjustments. In order to live lives that really matter, we have to do *things* that really matter.

98. Delegate responsibility and authority. One of the best ways for people to grow is by trying new things, doing new things and making a few mistakes along the way. If you are committed to building people in the organization, you need to make a habit of "passing the baton." We can have a tendency to over commit and do everything ourselves. When we learn how to delegate authority and responsibility, we develop future leaders and relieve some of our own workloads.

99. STOP WAITING! Start making the changes you need to – now! Most people have things they know need to change or improve but often procrastinate. We say things like *I'll begin right after the first of the year … I'll do it as soon as I finish this project … I'll work on it when things calm down.* Well, as the saying goes, "There's no time like the present." Pick one change you've been waiting to make – and stop waiting. Work on it today!

100. Embrace occasional failure! Take a risk and step outside of your comfort zone. Volunteer for a special extra assignment. Accept the responsibility of a new area. A client of mine once said he was "failing forward." We learn as much from our failures as we do from our successes. If you are not as successful as you would like to be, it might be because you are not trying enough new things – and occasionally failing along the way.

101. Reframe "missing the mark"! Instead of looking at something as a failure, try viewing it as an opportunity to improve and adjust what you do. A plane frequently slips off course on a flight from San Francisco to Hawaii. It is constantly getting feedback from towers and radar – and readjusting. Consider failure as valuable feedback to help you become the "best possible you."

102. Read books on successful people who failed many times before achieving great success ... Thomas Edison, Mary Kay Ash, Colonel Sanders, Roger Bannister – all committed and successful people who failed a lot! We don't remember them for their failures; we remember the successes that came from the feedback of their failures!

At age 22 – He failed in business
At age 23 – He ran for the Legislature and was defeated
At age 24 – He failed in business, once again
At age 29 – He was defeated for Speaker of The House
At age 34 – He was defeated for Congress
At age 39 – He lost another bid for Congress
At age 46 – He was defeated for the Senate
At age 47 – He was defeated for Vice President
At age 49 – He was again defeated for the Senate
At age 51 – He was elected President of The United States

He was ... **Abraham Lincoln**

103. Commit to removing one or more barriers from your past that may be hindering your future! Take a look at the following list of common roadblocks to leadership/personal effectiveness and identify any that you feel might have a negative hold on your life and your career.

- Fear of taking risks
- Lack of commitment
- Hero mentality
- Victim mentality
- Indecisiveness
- Low expectations of others
- Fear of failure
- Close-mindedness
- Overly critical
- Lack of focus

- Fear of being disliked
- Low self-esteem
- Low self-confidence
- Need for control
- Having to be perfect
- Fear of rejection
- High stress
- Fear of embarrassment
- Lack of endurance
- Low trust of others

Consider what is holding you back from being even more successful than you are now. For each of the items above that you identified, answer these questions:

*How has this barrier impacted my career and my life ...
what has it kept me from accomplishing?*

*When I get this out of my life, what will I be able
to have or accomplish?*

104. Learn the value of persistence. Identify something that, up until now, has gotten the best of you. Is there a person, a situation or a task that you have attempted to deal with but you have not been successful? Identify why the adversity is important to accomplish or overcome. Then, commit to be successful – no matter how many times you have to do it! One of the qualities of a good leader/person is the ability to pick yourself up, dust yourself off and try again! Persistence is best learned in the arena of life! How badly do you want something? Are you committed? Then try it again, until you get the results you desire!

47

105. Reflect on times when you didn't think you would or could accomplish something, but you did. Think of projects or opportunities that seemed overwhelming or unachievable – but you accomplished them anyway. Now that you are remembering how past commitment paid off, identify a new opportunity to add to this list! What is in front of you that you have not gone after or that you quit on because you didn't think you could be successful? Picture it in your mind and commit to pursue it with everything you have!

106. Identify what commitment looks like in your work environment. How can you and your team demonstrate commitment in daily interactions? Send out a one-page email asking for input from your team on how commitment shows up at work. Is it someone coming in twenty minutes early and being properly prepared for a successful day? Is it doing whatever it takes to finish a project on schedule? How might you demonstrate more commitment today? Once ideas have been collected, ask the team to commit to bringing those ideas to life. You go first!

> *Desire is the key to motivation, but it's determination and commitment to an unrelenting pursuit of your goal – a commitment to excellence – that will enable you to attain the success you seek.*

> ~ Mario Andretti

107. Create a "Growth Group." Establish a group of people within your organization and exchange books and CDs. What's in your personal library that might benefit a colleague, peer or direct report? There is so much great information out there that can help everyone. The more you share, the more there is to go around. The more that goes around, the more successful everyone will be.

108. Arrange for a motivational/inspirational speaker to present to the members of your team. And be sure to allow family members to attend as well. In fact, *encourage* their participation! A family that grows together stays together. As leaders, we need to be committed to helping our employees and coworkers experience positive personal lives. When people are struggling at home, it can impact the work they do … and the team members they do it with.

109. Create a reading club with some of your associates. When learning is done with a group of people, it can be fun and improves the entire team. Find three to ten individuals who want to grow and improve themselves. Acquire a few books in the field of leadership or personal development and have the group decide which one to review first. Have weekly meetings – either in person or via the internet. Talk about what you have learned and discuss ideas for implementing the ideas presented. This is a great way to heighten each participant's commitment to growth and development.

110. Organize a social get-together away from work. Sporting events, potluck dinners and game nights are great opportunities to strengthen relationships with members of your team and build greater commitment to each other's success. Getting to know each other better as people can have a positive impact on the communication and cooperation you experience within your work group. Make it happen. Find reasons to socialize outside of work.

111. Create an "Enemies List." As the saying goes: *You can tell a lot about people based on their friends. You can also tell a lot about them based on their enemies.* Successful people have many common enemies: "Average", "Good 'Nuff", "Denial", Playing "the Blame Game", etc. Post the list for all to see. Then, commit to doing your best to eliminate those destructive predators – and encourage others to do the same.

112. Maximize your time. Keep a daily activity log for an entire week. Record what you do and the time you spend doing it. At the end of the week, analyze the data. Look for patterns. Are you busy? Are you productive? If it's both, great! Keep doing what you're doing. If you find that you're really busy but not all that productive, some changes definitely are in order. Fact is, none of us were hired for the primary purpose of staying busy – we were hired to get things done!

Speaking of time …

113. Move beyond punctual. This month, commit to arriving ten minutes early for all meetings and appointments. Doing so demonstrates respect for others' time, shows people you are dependable and gives you some extra moments to prepare and get organized. You'll be ready for business the second the activity starts and better able to contribute to the desired outcome. And you just might find that any stress levels you normally experience are reduced significantly.

114. Go on an "in-office vacation." Isolate yourself for a day (or a large portion of one) to work on critical, high-priority tasks and projects. Ask others to handle things as if you really aren't there. Clear it with your manager. Explain what you'll be working on and its importance to the organization, and ask for his or her cooperation in honoring your "time off." Make sure that YOU act like you're not there by eliminating phone calls, socialization, etc. If you make a commitment to get something important done, it's up to you to create circumstances that allow you to live up to that commitment.

If we take care of the moments,
the years will take care of themselves.

~ Maria Edgeworth

115. Learn a language – either yours or a new one! Learning keeps the mind young. And language skills broaden our possibilities. Expand your English vocabulary by adding a new word daily. Dictionary.com has a "word of the day." Jot it down, review the definition and then use it five times that day. Once you do, it will be in your memory bank. Consider learning or advancing your skills in a language other than English. Most people admire others who are multilingual – especially when we're vacationing with them in a "foreign" land.

116. Commit to acquiring a missing personality quality that you desire. Perhaps you'd like to be more patient or more open-minded to different ideas. Maybe you'd like to bounce back from disappointment more quickly or accept criticism more constructively. Take an inventory of your personality and ask, "What trait do I desire that I lack?" Pick a time – a day, a weekend, a week – and focus on that quality. Notice how that quality manifests itself in specific behaviors of others. Adopt those same behaviors in your daily interactions and notice the positive results that come with them.

117. Commit to supporting your coworkers. Focus on "being there" for someone on your team – outside of the normal work environment. There are many times when associates or their family members will be facing difficult situations. Demonstrate understanding and compassion. Ask how you can help them make it through this tough time. Allow some schedule flexibility. Rearrange staffing so that their work is covered. Be available as a sounding board – someone to talk with … someone who will listen. Let the Golden Rule concept serve as your best behavioral guideline: support others in need as you would have them support you.

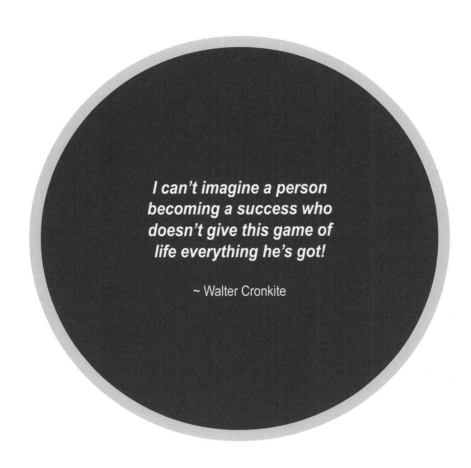

I can't imagine a person becoming a success who doesn't give this game of life everything he's got!

~ Walter Cronkite

Chapter 5

VISION:
I Have a Dream …

*Well, the future's always looked bleak 'til people with brains
and faith and courage who dreamed and dared to take great
risks found a way to make it better ….*

*If we're free to dare – and we are – if we're free to give –
and we are – then we're free to shape the future and have
within our grasp all that we dream that future will be.*

~ President Ronald Reagan

Would you depart on a weekend trip without knowing where you are
going? Would you board a plane with no idea where it was heading?
Would you set sail on a boat that had no rudder? Most folks would
respond to each of those questions with a resounding, NO WAY!
But ironically, many of those same people are doing the equivalent,
every day, as they run their businesses and live their lives.

Career studies indicate that, typically, more planning
goes into our VAcations than our VOcations!

In his best-selling book *The 7 Habits of Highly Effective People,* Dr. Stephen Covey teaches us to "begin with the end in mind" – a guiding principle I have recommended a few times throughout this work. A lot of people, however, do just the opposite – they start in the here and now and move towards some "tomorrow" that is neither clearly defined nor envisioned. Then, all too frequently, they experience varying degrees of fear and doubt, they stumble a few times and then they throw in the towel – refocusing on that here and now as if that is all there is. The underlying problem: Their visions aren't clear enough ... they're not real enough. THEY HAVE STOPPED DREAMING!

Roger Bannister had a vision to run faster than a four-minute mile. It was thought impossible, but Roger never let other people's limited reality discourage him. In 1954, he ran a sub-four-minute mile. Within forty-six days, his record was broken – and within a year, numerous people had run the mile in less than four minutes. But Roger was the first. He not only broke the time record, he also broke the *belief* barrier because he had a vision ... he had a dream!

Who can forget the famous *I Have a Dream* speech by Dr. Martin Luther King? He said, "I have a dream that my four little children will one day live in a nation where they will not be judged by the color of their skin, but by the content of their character. I have a *dream* today."

Franklin Delano Roosevelt said, "The only limits to our realization of tomorrow will be our doubts of today." When you have a vision – when you are stirred by a dream – then you are working towards something special. **Living a life that matters begins with a dream to do so!**

118. Get up 30 minutes early and visualize the successful day you are going to have. Choose what type of day it will be. Envision the "perfect day" and choose to make it happen. The choices we make every day determine the type of lives we will have. Prepare to make adjustments as circumstances present themselves. Create a vision for a wonderful and positive day.

119. Visualize your "shots." Golf legend Jack Nicklaus pictures each shot in his mind – before making it. He stands behind the ball, imagines himself swinging and making contact, and then "sees" the ball traveling to the desired location. Only then does he take his stance and begin the actual shot. He knows what success looks like – what his target is – before taking action to get there. And his lifelong record speaks for itself. So take a lesson from one of the best of the best. Before you begin any activity, create a vision of you doing it as well as it can be done. Picture your success first, and you'll know what your target is – and you'll increase your chances of hitting the mark every time.

120. Ask your coworkers about *their* visions … their dreams, and reciprocate by sharing yours. Doing so is an excellent way to learn about each other, strengthen relationships and discover things you have in common.

121. Reflect on the values that you admire in others around you. Think about those values and how they are demonstrated. Then answer this question:

What can/will I do to adopt those behaviors I most admire?

122. Take a moment and write out your definition of success. Nobody else can define that end state for you except you. If you don't have a definition of success, how can you determine if you are on or off course? If you lived the life you were supposed to, how would you know?

123. Start a vision album. Get a photo album, a three-ring binder or a simple office folder and start collecting images of your dreams. Whenever you see a magazine photo that connects with (or reminds you of) something important in your life, tear it out and put it in the album. If you read a newspaper article about someone you admire and wish to be like, cut it out and put it in the album. Let your album build over time – and review it frequently to stay focused on the visions for your life.

124. Define success in the beginning – measure it at the end. Whenever you start a meeting, project, intervention or group activity, ask all participants to complete this sentence:

This activity will be successful if we …..

Based on the input, create a master list of "success criteria" that everyone agrees with. Include how you will work together as well as what you will accomplish. Once the work is completed, pull out the list and evaluate your results. Did you accomplish what you wanted? Did you match your definitions of success? If yes, celebrate! If no, keep working until you do!

125. See it in the news. For your next project – individually or as a team – write out a press release about the successful completion of the project. Script out a news reporter's interview about the incredible way you accomplished your feat. What impact has it had on the industry, on your team, your community? Begin with the end in mind and make it as vivid as possible, which makes it real. Be careful … you might get more excited about the task at hand and exceed your expectations!

126. Get rid of your baggage. What is it that bothers you the most? What's your biggest gripe? Picture it in your mind. Got it? Great. Now here's what you need to do: FORGETABOUTIT! Move on. Put it in your past. Decide to let it go. You really can, you know. Being bothered is a response we choose. So is refusing to let things get us down.

A vision is not just a picture of what could be; it is an appeal to our better selves, a call to become something more.

~ Rosabeth Moss Kanter

127. Question authority – starting with YOURS! Do some self-reflection, and see if your behaviors are in sync with your vision of good leadership. Ask yourself questions like:
Do I make a sincere effort to manage for the good of everyone?
Do I do what I do because I truly believe it is right?
Am I committed to being the best leader I can be?

128. Evaluate your impact. Before going to sleep, replay your day and think about how your interactions impacted others. Consider what type of example you provided. Were you a positive role model? Did your behaviors create an image of someone your coworkers would want to emulate – or someone they wouldn't? Are you totally satisfied with the YOU people saw and experienced today?

129. Build a better environment. At the start of each week, imagine the perfect working environment for you and your colleagues. What does it look and feel like? How are people behaving and interacting? Once you have that vision in place, identify one thing you can and will do that week to help make that vision a reality. Write it down. Keep it where you will see it. DO IT! At the end of the year, you will have made 45–50 contributions to a better workplace.

Here are some ideas to get you started …

130. Use voice mail and email to encourage people and build them up. Leave a message expressing your appreciation for their hard work, assistance, understanding – whatever the situation dictates. Consider doing it in the evening or on weekends so that they will start their very next work day knowing they are valued and appreciated.

131. Call them by name. When talking with people, use their names. Doing so makes your communication more personal. And it's a sign that you recognize them as individuals rather than mere cogs in the business wheel.

132. Pay attention to your body language and the messages it may be sending. Only 7% of communication is done through words; 93% is everything else (voice tone and gestures). A picture is worth a thousand words. Stand confidently. Maintain eye contact with those to whom you are speaking. Avoid distracting gestures such as tapping your fingers, crossing your arms or rolling your eyes. And periodically examine your communication habits to make sure that your physical gestures are in sync with your words and intended messages.

133. Practice "The 3 F's" of compassionate communication.
1. "I understand how you Feel."
2. "I've Felt that before myself."
3. "What I have Found is …."

When people are struggling with difficult challenges, the sincere use of these 3 F's can soothe their stress, demonstrate that you're listening and that you care, and enhance the trust level that exists between you.

134. Pursue clarity. If a person says something you don't understand, ask for clarification in a non-challenging way. Saying things like "Scott, I'm not sure I really understand what you're saying. Could you go over that again?" or "How do you see that working?" or "I'm not all that familiar with what happened. Can you fill me in a little?" not only fosters more effective communication but also encourages the speaker to keep talking.

135. Reinforce the values and visions using technology. Find short web "viral" movies that reinforce important organizational values or positive visions for the future and share them with everyone on your team. View and discuss them during meetings and at the start of team projects. It's a great way to keep the things that are truly important in front of people. (Looking for some movies you can view right away? Check out *www.walkthetalk.com*.)

136. Enlist your team members in a "Values Patrol." Ask for everyone's commitment to tell each other (including you) whenever they observe actions or decisions that are out of sync with organizational or team values … when the group is not living up to their own vision of what they stand for and how they intend to operate. Make this a fun activity. Consider appointing a Values Officer for important meetings on a rotational basis. Give the person a toy police badge and whistle to blow when "violators" are spotted.

137. Celebrate success BEFORE you achieve it. Have an awards ceremony for your team's success at the beginning of a project or when a new "push" is announced. Begin with the end in mind. Get excited about what happens on the other side of success and notice how you and the team can't wait to get back there for real.

138. Include *"in a way that."* When planning your activities, write down what you intend to accomplish, then add the phrase "in a way that contributes to and supports my/our vision." Once you've made your specific plans, go back and check them against this add-on criteria. Remember that everything you do either brings your dreams closer to reality or moves them farther away. Choose the former!

139. Dream your dimes away. Review your activities and accomplishments at the end of each day. How many of them moved you a little closer to the vision you have for your life and career? Write that number down, and put that many dimes in a pickle jar. Do this every day. Once your jar is full, donate all the money to a charity so they can move closer to their vision as well.

140. Be passionate about your dreams for yourself, your team and your organization. Let your excitement show. Let your pride ooze out for all to see. Celebrate each step that moves you closer to your desired end state. Reinforce and sincerely thank those who make those steps possible. Encourage others to bounce back from setbacks and disappointments with a big smile and an even bigger helping hand. Believe in your cause. Believe in your dreams. Most importantly, BELIEVE IN YOURSELF!

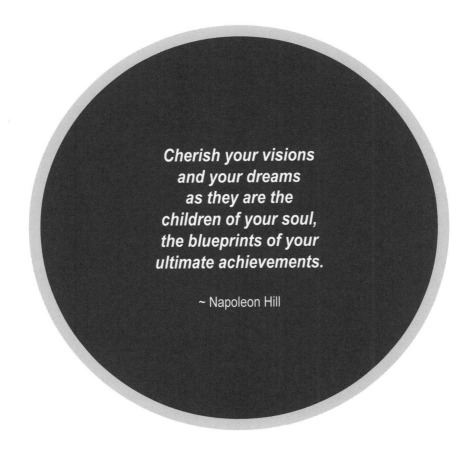

*Cherish your visions
and your dreams
as they are the
children of your soul,
the blueprints of your
ultimate achievements.*

~ Napoleon Hill

Chapter 6

TEAMWORK:
There IS an "I" in Team!

*One piece of log creates a small fire adequate to warm you up.
Add just a few more pieces to blast an immense bonfire large
enough to warm up your entire circle of friends. Needless to say
that individuality counts, but teamwork dynamites.*

~ Jin Kwon

Success is a "team sport." You don't achieve it alone – and even if you
could, you probably wouldn't want to enjoy and celebrate it by yourself.
Living your life like it matters is about living a successful life … about
making it across the finish line of life. My goal – as a teacher, author,
father, friend and human being – is to help as many people as I can
across that finish line called success. A party of one is not much of a
party at all.

As I mentioned earlier, there are many misconceptions floating around
out there – concepts that are widely accepted as truths but really aren't
so. Since everything we do (or don't do) is driven by our belief systems,
we need to identify these misconceptions for what they are: bogus. One
of the bigger misconceptions I've come across is one I'm sure you've also
heard: **"There is no 'I' in TEAM."** I believe that to be false. Now I know
technically (grammatically) it is accurate, but from a practical standpoint
it's way off base. If there is no "I" in team, then there is also no "U" in it.
And if there is no "U" in TEAM, then there is no team – unless you are
talking about someone *else's* team.

I've had the good fortune to work with many successful teams that include professional athletes, NFL football players and world record holders in Olympic sports. I've also worked with scores of successful corporate teams like Kraft, Nabisco, MillerCoors, Cintas (the uniform company) and Cingular. One of the many things all of these groups have in common is an unwavering belief in the validity of the old saying ...

Together Everyone Achieves More

For them, that phrase is more than just a "saying" (or a cliché); it's a way of life ... a guiding principle for success.

A while back, I had a senior executive from one of the world's largest and best-known soft drink companies in one of my classes. Midway through the session he made a statement I'll never forget. He said, "Mr. Black, we are not in the sugar water business. We are in the *people* business. We just sell sugar water to make a profit." What a great perspective on the importance of people and the teams they comprise.

Take a moment and think about some people who have had a positive impact on others – individuals who have lived lives that matter. How many of them did it all by themselves? The answer should be obvious: NONE OF THEM! They all relied on "teams" of people to multiply and maximize their legacy of greatness. They needed others to reach their true potential, **and so do you.**

Truly successful people know that they must build, support, nurture and encourage teams – and be contributing members of them. You'll find a collection of strategies for doing that on the pages that follow.

141. Create incentive programs that include family members (or close friends). Recognition and rewards that involve actual relatives often produce more of a sense of family in the workplace. I love working in the *Machillas* in Mexico. The work environment is very "familia" oriented. They have frequent family days, picnics and other events that bring people together and create stronger coworker bonds.

142. Identify the qualities and characteristics of a High-Performance Team. Consider your team functioning at its highest level. What would it look like? How would it feel? What behaviors would be prevalent? Have a meeting to collect input from team members and work together to create a master list. Post the list around the office or work area the week after the meeting to keep the team focused on those qualities. *Then …*

143. Categorize those qualities as either "Skills" or "Attitudes." In a different meeting, preferably the next one, bring the list back and get the group involved in determining which ones are skill-related and which ones are attitudinal. In all likelihood, the majority of the items will fall into the attitude arena. When the work is completed, pose these two questions to the group:

1. What did you learn/discover from this exercise?
2. What, specifically, can we do to apply that learning?

144. Find out what behaviors you are promoting (or discouraging). Ask a couple of people you work with to help you identify the actions and behaviors that you are reinforcing. Do you acknowledge when something is done right? Do you only speak up when there is a problem? Do you encourage open communication? Do you have a tendency to "shoot the messenger"? Behaviors are the products of their consequences. So examine the consequences you provide and commit to eliminating any that are counterproductive to team effectiveness.

145. Team up away from the job. Organize a few coworkers and make a contribution in your community. Get involved with things like road and neighborhood cleaning, canned food drives, blood drives, etc. Wear caps or T-shirts displaying your organization's logo. Get involved multiple times throughout the year – not just during "the holidays." Remember that your team has a "life" of its own. Do your part to make sure that life matters!

146. Take care of "your own." Put together a fund for a team member who is struggling financially. Volunteer to cover the shift of a coworker who needs time to care for an ailing relative. Lend an automobile to a colleague who has lost his or her transportation. Lots of people are struggling these days. Pay attention to chatter in your work groups or at the water cooler. How might you be a force for helping someone on a personal level? When people know they are cared for, they will commit even more to the team. See how you might inspire others to extend a helping hand to a fellow team member in need.

147. Invest in your team members. Make a commitment to reach out and help somebody who is struggling with a task or project. Seizing opportunities to contribute to others' success is one of many ways to live a life that matters.

There is no such thing as a self-made man. You reach your goals only with the help of others.

~ George Shinn

148. Get to know your coworkers. Study after study shows that the better people know each other, the more they like each other – and the more they like each other, the more effectively they work together. How well do you know the people you work with? Is anybody having a baby? Who has a sick friend? Whose spouse is out of work? Who is celebrating a birthday or anniversary?

149. Make the most of your "rewarding" opportunities. When you have the chance to present someone with an award, or offer a public acknowledgment of merit, DO IT! Find out what's important to the people around you and use that information to make them feel special. Make sure it is deserved, sincere and specific to that person. When you are specific about the recognition and personalize the "payoff," the effect is powerful and lasting.

150. Don't wait! Give recognition as soon as possible after the good performance takes place. Praise tends to lose its effectiveness with the passing of time.

151. When you bring on new team members ask them, "How do you like to be rewarded when you do a great job?" This will help you know what motivates each person – and it also creates the expectation of doing good work.

152. Make it sweet. Bring in a special snack or finger food for your team. Providing a treat can make everyone's day a bit more special. Having something special like cookies, brownies or cupcakes can add a little sweetness to a normal routine. People may not need the calories but they will appreciate the thought.

153. Show a little consideration. Remember that your workplace is a shared environment. Set a considerate example by doing things like cleaning up after yourself, sharing equipment and resources, and respecting others' time by not interrupting them or expecting them to drop what they are doing every time you need something.

154. Got a problem? Go to the source! People can't fix problems they don't know about, nor are they likely to discontinue disturbing behaviors if they don't know that others are bothered. So whenever you have an issue with someone on the team, talk to him or her about it. But never, ever whine about it or complain to others. The issue is between the two of you, so keep it that way. Talking things through in a respectful manner is the best way to solve problems and maintain relationships.

155. Embrace diversity. No two people are exactly the same. Each of us is unique and special. So, work on accepting and appreciating team members who are "different." Without question, workforce diversity is a significant business advantage. Teams that are true "melting pots" (demographically, culturally and intellectually) have a greater ability to understand and meet the needs of a diverse marketplace – and they're significantly better equipped to make a positive difference.

156. This one bears repeating: CELEBRATE SUCCESS! Find ways to celebrate the big and small successes in your life. Too often, we push hard for a goal or a deadline only to find that another is right in front of us. Stop and savor each accomplishment – both individually and as a team. Make it big or make it small, just be sure you make it happen.

157. Empower others to lead. Encourage more team members to step forward and assume leadership roles. Are there people in your group who would be great at heading up projects, making important presentations to key members of management and the like? Encourage them to step forward, give them a little nudge, coach them, support them and watch them flourish. They will feel extra special, and you will be adding more value to the people who matter in your life.

158. Share your spotlight. Remember those who have helped you be successful. When you are recognized for doing great work, mention and thank those behind the scenes or your peers who contributed to your success. In his famous poem "For Whom the Bell Tolls," John Donne reminds us that "No man is an island, entire of itself: each is a piece of the continent, a part of the main." Acknowledge those who help *you* get acknowledged and notice how much better the team functions!

159. Remove their obstacles. Ask each member of your team to identify the two or three most significant obstacles negatively impacting their performance (e.g., faulty equipment, unclear instructions, prohibitive policies, poor interdepartmental cooperation, etc.). Create a master list and start working to eliminate as many of the obstacles as you can. Just minimizing a few of them can make a HUGE difference for everyone on the team.

160. Don't punish good performers. Most leaders tend to rely on their best people to handle tough assignments to get them through difficult situations. That's both natural and potentially problematic. "You did such a great job handling that lousy situation; the next time we have one we'll be calling on you again." Sound familiar? Unless people *want* all the tough stuff, being a victim of their own competence can be very demotivating. So spread that "tough stuff" around, or at least make it worthwhile for team members to take on more than their fair share.

161. Be someone's cheerleader. Most people have a need for others to believe in them and cheer them on. So, this week, identify someone for whom you can be a cheerleader. Encourage them; root them on. Let them know you believe in them or how proud you are of them. When people know you believe in them, they start believing in themselves, and everybody accomplishes more!

162. Tell your "secrets." Share information about what makes you successful. Pass along any "tricks of the trade" that you've learned over time, and ask your team members to reciprocate. When everyone learns and grows together, EVERYONE WINS!

Similarly …

163. Become a mentor. Reach out to someone new or a colleague who is struggling and help them … coach them … mentor them. Some organizations have structured mentoring programs. If one exists where you work, get involved. If you don't have such a program, GET INVOLVED elsewhere! When you give of yourself you are making an impact that is immeasurable – and living a life that truly matters.

164. Get in the habit of asking "What do YOU think?" When team members' ideas are solicited and considered, they tend to develop more of an ownership mentality. There's more buy-in … more engagement. Employees that "own" their jobs approach them differently. They are more committed to their organizations, to their leaders and to each other.

None of us is as smart as ALL of us.

~ Ken Blanchard

165. Tell on someone. Keep your eyes and ears open for examples of outstanding service, attitude or assistance provided by people outside of your team. Then tell *their* managers about them. See how many people you can get recognized for extra effort. You'll be amazed at the impact you can create with a little "tattling."

166. Eliminate "it's not my job" from your vocabulary (and from your thinking). When you see something that needs to be done, DO IT – even if it doesn't fall within your direct responsibility. Ensuring mutual success requires initiative and action – not job description enforcement.

68

167. Give someone permission to be great today! Compliment someone; help a person in need; listen to someone on your team;
inject some enthusiasm or passion. Do it for the value of the
act itself and for the benefit of others who may be watching.
As leaders we give people permission through our own actions.

168. Let them vent. Be a sounding board for team members who may
occasionally need to unload. Keep an open door. Encourage
them to come to you with issues and concerns. Often just having
"a shoulder to cry on" is all that is needed to relieve tension and
get back on track. Stress is a definite roadblock to success. Help
ease it and you've done the person, and yourself, a huge favor.

169. Arrange for – and participate in – periodic team-building events
and activities. Do some research on the Internet to locate firms
that specialize in that field. Check with your HR department to see
what may be available in-house. Purchase a collection of short
group exercises that can be done during meetings and "brown-
bag seminars." The more you practice, the better you'll be.

170. Get your team together and create a "worry list." Even though
worries are often unfounded, they still result in negative energy
and fear that can sometimes paralyze people. It's difficult to be *in*
the now moment and remain focused when one is preoccupied
with worry. Once you create the list, have a shredding ceremony.
Read each concern aloud, have the team say in unison, "Good-
bye, worry," and pass it through the shredder. Try it! You'll be
amazed at how effective this symbolic gesture can be.

171. Remember the team at home. Use some of your vacation days or
other available leave to spend time with, and nurture, your family.
We all need balance in our lives. Most of us work very hard. By
making sure that our family lives are positive and healthy, we help
ourselves to be better team members at work. We can't live our
lives like they matter without focusing on the people who matter
most in our lives.

172. Take new team members under your wing. People come and go. Teams lose members and get new ones. Be the one who welcomes new team members, introduces them to the group and orients them to how things work. It can be uncomfortable being the "new kid on the block." Getting started can be awkward. You can minimize that by stepping up and doing whatever you can to help facilitate a smooth transition.

173. Work on understanding others before expecting to be understood. Set a personal goal to listen twice as much as you talk. Make a habit of restating to people the messages you believe they are conveying. Pay attention to the body language that others exhibit. Explore the messages behind the messages. Explain what you are hearing, seeing and reading – and confirm that you "get" their point.

174. When it comes to teams and teamwork, think ACHIEVE:

> **A**ccept and meet all of your responsibilities.
> **C**ontribute to everyone's success.
> **H**elp others develop and grow.
> **I**nfect everyone with "contagious enthusiasm."
> **E**mbrace diversity and change.
> **V**erbalize your dreams ... and your appreciation.
> **E**xpect the best – and give it yourself!

175. Be human. Open yourself up to your team. Let them see that you are more than an employee, a supervisor or a boss. Share your dreams and your hopes – and your fears. Let others know who you are and what is important to you. Team members will come to realize that you share many similarities – and you really are ALL in this together.

176. Measure what you seek. Team members tend to judge what's truly important by looking at what is monitored and measured – and what isn't. Take a moment to examine your "scorecards." Are you collecting data on ALL the things you say are important? Do you provide feedback on ALL the behaviors and activities that matter for your group? You increase everyone's success potential when you INspect what you EXpect.

177. Keep them "in the loop." People need information in order to meet their responsibilities and your expectations. So get them the data they need. Let them know the *whats* and *whens* of things that must be done. More importantly, tell them the *WHYS*. Review any requirements that must be met and restrictions that must be followed. Knowledge is power. When you keep people informed, you empower them to do their very best work.

178. Here's a simple yet powerfully profound guideline for your team, your job, your career and your life:

> **The only way you EARN the right to expect things of others is by doing those same things yourself.**

179. Perform with integrity. Demonstrate your personal commitment to ethical behavior. Follow the rules. Honor your commitments. Do what's right rather than what's easy and convenient. Be honest and respectful. Carry your share of the load. Evaluate everything you do, and plan to do, by answering one simple question:

Will the people I care about most be proud of me?

180. Make sure the invisible sign that describes you continues to read "UNDER CONSTRUCTION." Recommit to ongoing learning and growth. Reread this book frequently and identify new action items to practice – for yourself and your team. Choose to make today better than yesterday and tomorrow better than today. Encourage everyone you work with to step outside their comfort zone and

live *their* lives like they matter!

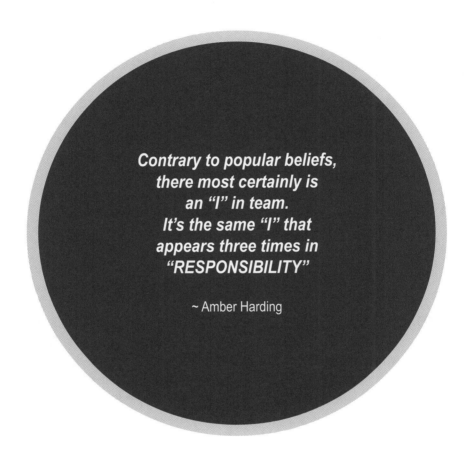

*Contrary to popular beliefs,
there most certainly is
an "I" in team.
It's the same "I" that
appears three times in
"RESPONSIBILITY"*

~ Amber Harding

Closing Thoughts

Over the years, I've been given many valuable gifts.

I've been blessed with a wealth of opportunities to learn and grow through my own personal experiences – and through the experiences of others. And I've tried my best to pass those gifts along to you by sharing what I have found to be the keys to individual success:

Passion, Purpose, Focus,
Commitment, Vision and *Teamwork*

They are the foundation for doing anything great. They are the roadmap for living a life that matters.

Yes, this book is my gift to you. But there is one string attached … one caveat to heed and remember:

The information presented in these pages is intended to be PRACTICED – not merely READ!

So I encourage you to use this book as a "workbook." Mark it up, high-light it, write in it, circle stuff and connect multiple "ways" with lines to create an overall strategy for action. Now that you've read it through once, go back and select one or two chapters you want to start working on and GET STARTED!

Consider purchasing a blank journal (or something similar) or add a blank section to your day planner. Use it to keep an ongoing record of your thoughts, to document the many "make-a-list" exercises in this book and to track your plans, activities and goals. Think of it as your *Book of Success*.

Choose to make the action items in this book part of your daily routine. Make them goals to achieve and pursue them with everything you have. You control your own life and career. You have the "stop" and "go" buttons in your hand. Hit the GO button!

Engage your mind. Engage your body. ENGAGE YOUR HEART!
We all get one shot at life. Make yours a great one.

I have been all over the world, and no matter the country, no matter the language, I've always found that there are certain universal truths. Truth transcends philosophy, language and even political ideology. As I journey across this planet, I know that two plus two always equals four – regardless of my longitude or latitude. I know that water will be wet, snow will be cold and fire will warm wherever I am. And I've come to learn another universal truth that hopefully will inspire you as much as it has me:

When you live your life like it matters, it DOES!

With Passion – Heart, Body and Soul

Scott J. Black

When I was a young man,
I wanted to change the world.

I found it was difficult to change the world,
so I tried to change my nation.

When I found I couldn't change the nation,
I began to focus on my town.

I couldn't change the town, and as an older man,
I tried to change my family.

Now, as an old man, I realize the only thing
I can change is myself, and suddenly I realize
that if long ago I had changed myself,
I could have made an impact on my family.

My family and I could have made
an impact on our town.

Their impact could have changed the nation and

I could indeed have changed the world.

(Author unknown)

The Author

Scott V. Black is a passion generator. His mission is getting people emotionally involved in their personal causes and helping individuals and organizations reach their true potential.

He is a human motivator committed to passionately challenging leaders to be "under construction."

He is the author of **Becoming Your Dreams: Want it. Create it. Live it.** Along with notables such as Jim Rohn and Dr. Warren Bennis, Scott was a contributing author to **Yes You Can! Reaching Your Potential While Achieving Greatness**. He's also the coauthor of **Discover Your Inner Strength** – with Stephen Covey and Ken Blanchard.

Scott's company, **Empower U International**, offers the most powerful leadership training available today. Empower U's Transformational Leadership Training encourages individuals and corporations to raise the bar and become the best of the best. His clients include MillerCoors, TPI Composites, Kraft – and hundreds of other national and international companies.

Learn more about how you can take your company, your career and your life to new levels of passion, purpose and profitability by visiting **www.EmpowerU.net**.

> "I owe everything to God. He is the great creator, and all that I have presented in this work flows from him."
>
> ~ Scott V. Black

The Publisher

For over 30 years, WalkTheTalk.com has been dedicated to one simple goal…one single mission: *To provide you and your organization with high-impact resources for your personal and professional success.*

Walk The Talk resources are designed to:

- Develop your skills and confidence
- Inspire your team
- Create customer enthusiasm
- Build leadership skills
- Stretch your mind
- Handle tough "people problems"
- Develop a culture of respect and responsibility
- And, most importantly, help you achieve your personal and professional goals.

Contact the Walk The Talk team at
1.888.822.9255
or visit us at www.walkthetalk.com

Resources for Personal and Professional Success

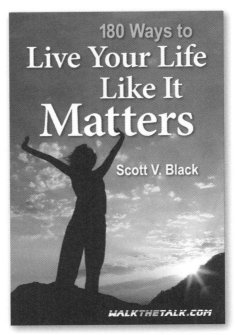

Available in 2 formats!

Softcover Book – $12.95   **Digital Format (ebook) – $9.95**

"This life we are living right now is not a practice game. It is the World Series, the Super Bowl, and the Olympics all rolled up into one. If you don't feel that kind of power and passion about whom you are and what you do, you need to start thinking in new ways. This book will give you 180 opportunities to change your thinking, your decisions, your actions, and your life."

Jim Stovall
Author of *The Ultimate Gift*

Order a copy for EVERYONE in your organization TODAY!

Visit

WALKTHETALK.COM

Resources for Personal and Professional Success

to purchase *180 Ways to Live Your Life Like It Matters* books or digital downloads.

Take yourself and your organization to the next level with

180 Ways to Live Your Life Like It Matters
Personal AND Professional Success Kit

$29.95

CONTAINS THE FOLLOWING RESOURCES:

- ■ A copy of *180 Ways to Live Your Life Like It Matters*
- ■ DVD containing:
  - • A 3-minute motivational movie that summarizes and reinforces the important *180 Ways to Live Your Life Like It Matters* principles

    Great meeting starter and training supplement!

  - • Individual learning exercises and action planner to enhance your personal performance and build your leadership legacy

    Effective self-development tools – just for you!

  - • Group discussion questions and learning exercises that encourage your organization team to follow and apply *180 Ways to Live Your Life Like It Matters* principles and strategies

    Perfect for team building and leadership development!

WALKTHETALK.COM

Resources for Personal and Professional Success

Visit
WALKTHETALK.COM
to learn more about our:

Leadership & Personal Development Center

- Develop leadership skills
- Motivate your team
- Achieve business results

Greenhouse Bookstore

- Save time
- Save money
- Save the planet

Free Newsletters

- Daily Inspiration
- The Power of Inspiration
- The Leadership Solution
- New Products and Special Offers

Motivational Gift Books

- Inspire your team
- Create customer enthusiasm
- Reinforce core values

**Contact the Walk The Talk team at 1.888.822.9255
or visit us at www.walkthetalk.com.**